CAMBRIDGE
UNIVERSITY PRESS

CAMBRIDGE ENGLISH
Language Assessm
Part of the University of Cam

STORYFUN 3

STUDENT'S BOOK

with Online Activities
and Home Fun Booklet 3
Second edition

Karen Saxby

Cambridge University Press
www.cambridge.org/elt

Cambridge Assessment English
www.cambridgeenglish.org

Information on this title: www.cambridge.org/9781316617151

© Cambridge University Press 2017

First published 2011
Second edition 2017

20 19 18 17 16 15 14 13 12 11

Printed in Dubai by Oriental Press

A catalogue record for this publication is available from the British Library

ISBN 978-1-316-61715-1 Student's Book with online activities and Home Fun booklet
ISBN 978-1-316-61718-2 Teacher's Book with Audio
ISBN 978-1-316-61721-2 Presentation Plus

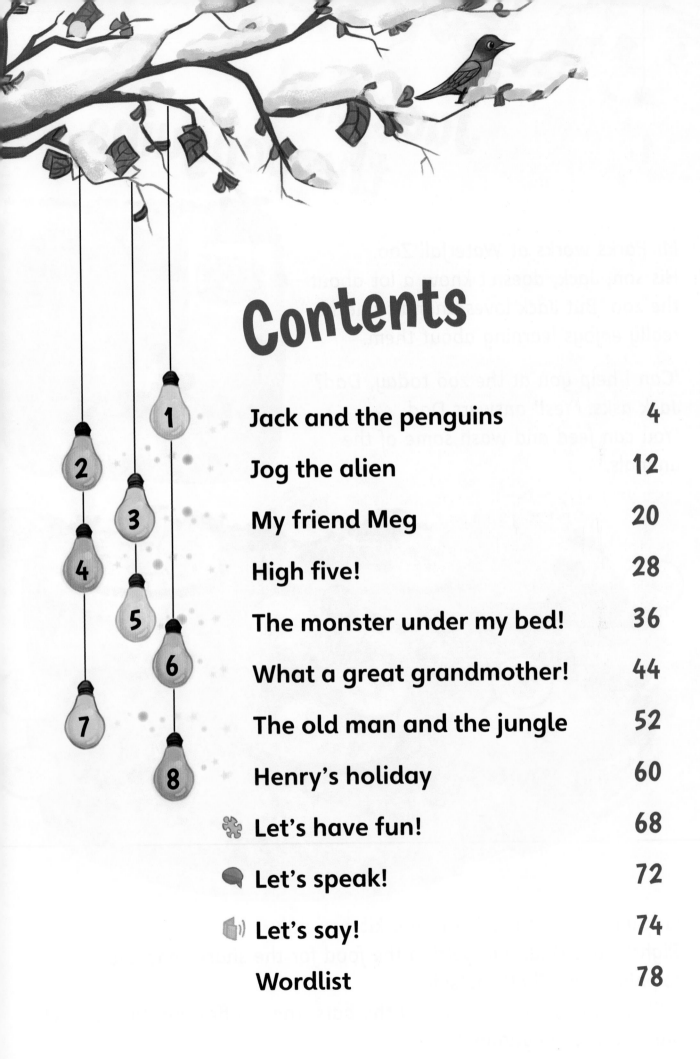

Contents

Jack and the penguins

Mr Parks works at Waterfall Zoo.
His son, Jack, doesn't know a lot about
the zoo. But Jack loves animals and he
really enjoys learning about them.

'Can I help you at the zoo today, Dad?'
Jack asks. 'Yes!' answers Dad.
'You can feed and wash some of the
animals.'

Jack and his dad are in the zoo kitchen now.
'Right!' says Dad. 'I'm getting the food for the sharks and the
dolphins now. That's outside.'
'OK!' Jack answers. 'Can I feed the bats, the giraffes and the zebras?
Oh! And the kangaroos?'

'No. Sorry, Jack. Feed our ten penguins first, please.'
'Great! I love penguins!' Jack says.
'Me too!' says his father. 'Their food is in that big grey cupboard.'
But Jack isn't looking in the big grey cupboard. He's looking in the
big blue cupboard.

He's looking at the fruit juice, the cheese, the watermelon, the
lemonade and at a big meat and potato pie.

'Which is the penguins' food?' Jack thinks. 'Oh dear! I don't know.
That pie?'

He thinks again. 'What do penguins really like eating?
Those grapes, these kiwis, those burgers, these sandwiches?'

Then Jack sees four milkshakes. 'The pie and these milkshakes, I
think. OK! How much pie and how many milkshakes for ten penguins?
Oh dear! I don't know.'

Jack picks up ALL the pie and ALL the milkshakes and carries everything carefully to the penguins.

'Are you hungry? Are you thirsty?' he calls and puts the pie and milkshakes on the ground. The penguins look at the pie and then look at the milkshakes and then look at Jack.

'Oh dear! You don't want the pie and you don't want the milkshakes,' says Jack and runs and gets the lemonade and sandwiches and puts them on the ground.

But the penguins don't look happy.

'Some water and some little fish?' he asks.
The penguins jump up and down, up and down.
Jack laughs and says, 'So, penguins like water and fish! I'm learning a lot today!'

Jack goes back to the kitchen. He puts some water in a big bowl and then finds the fish in the big grey cupboard.
'Twenty fish for ten little penguins. Great!' he says and carries everything carefully to the penguins.

The penguins look at the water and the fish and look at Jack and drink all the water and eat all the fish! 'Wow!' Jack thinks. 'I'm learning a lot today.'

He runs and tells his father. 'The penguins are fine now, Dad. Can I get a burger for the bats, some juice for the giraffes, some cheese for the zebras and some kiwis for the kangaroos now, please?'

Dad smiles. 'I think you looked in the wrong cupboard, Jack! That's not the food for our animals. Sorry! Come on. Let's go and get the right food now. I can help you learn all about the animals here. I know you love learning about them. Then we can wash the elephants. Elephants really enjoy that!'
'Do they? Wow!' says Jack!

I AM learning a lot today!

Jack and the penguins

A Find and write the words.

Food

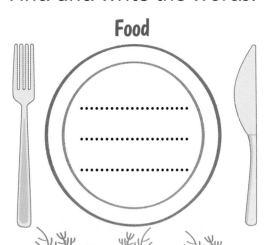

....

....

....

Sea animals

......shark......

....

....

sharksandwichesdolphinmilkshakewhalecheese

B Read and answer the questions.

1 What is the name of Jack's father?   ...Mr Parks...

2 What colour is the penguins' food cupboard?   ....

3 What is in the pie?   ....

4 How many fish does Jack take to the penguins?   ....

5 What does Jack want to give to the zebras?   ....

6 Which animals do Jack and his dad wash?   the ....

C Who's talking about the story? Tick (✔) the correct box.

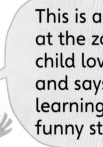

This is about a child at the zoo. The child loves animals and says, 'Wow, I'm learning a lot.' It's a funny story. ☐

This story is about some penguins. A boy says, 'Come and eat!' but the penguins don't like the boy. It's a sad story. ☐

D *How many?* or *How much*? Draw lines.

How many?   How much?

E Read about bats. Choose the right words.

Bats

1. You don't see bats ....*in*........ the morning
or afternoon. Bats fly and look for their food   in   off   to

2. .... night. Some people think bats   on   at   with

3. .... birds but that's wrong.   be   is   are

4. .... lot of bats like eating flies and spiders.   A   The   An
Some bats like eating fruit but baby bats drink milk.

5. .... get their milk from their mothers.   He   We   They

6. Bats .... very big ears!   has   have   having

F Ask and answer the questions. Read and say.

1 Do you like animals?

Yes, I love them!

2 Have you got a pet?

3 Would you like to go to a zoo?

Whales or snails? Dogs or frogs?

Monkeys or donkeys? Bats or cats?

What's your favourite animal?

G How many animal words can you make? You can use the letters more than once.

Jack is looking in the cupboard now.

..dog...

....

H Which one is different? Circle and say.

The shark! The shark can't walk but the zebra, elephant and goat can walk.

Those animals have legs, but that animal hasn't got legs.

1

2

3

4

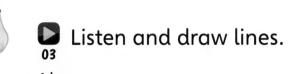

I 〔▶〕 Listen and draw lines.
03

Alex   Kim   Nick

Eva   Pat   Sally

J   Complete your story and zoo picture.

My day at the ZOO

My name's .... I'm at the zoo today. I'm taking photos
of the .... with my new phone. The animals are hungry
and thirsty. A boy is bringing them some .... and some
.... 'How .... do those
animals eat every day?' I ask the boy. 'Oh lots!' he says. 'And how
.... water do those animals drink every day?' I ask. 'Oh
lots!' he says. 'How .... do you eat and how
.... do you drink every day?' the boy asks
me. 'Oh lots!' I say.

p. 68

p. 72

Jog the alien

2

Jog is an alien. He's in Skiptown today. There are lots of exciting places in the town and Jog likes visiting exciting places! Jog is going into the supermarket in Green Street now. He wants some vegetables for his picnic.

Mr and Mrs Doors live in Green Street. They are in the bookshop. Mrs Doors points to Jog and says, 'There's an alien in our supermarket!' 'No, there isn't,' says Mr Doors. 'That's Charlie, I think. Yes, I think that's Charlie! Charlie likes wearing funny clothes. Hello, Charlie!' he calls.

'Good morning!' answers Jog. 'Shall I get you some beans?'
'No, thanks!' Mr Doors answers.
'What about an onion?' asks Jog. Aliens LOVE eating onions.
'No,' Mr Doors says. 'But thank you for asking, Charlie.'

Jog buys his vegetables and then goes to the car park in Skiptown. The car park is in the town centre. Jog sits and has his picnic and then counts the cars there. Aliens LOVE counting cars.

Charlie and Lily live in Skiptown. They're in the town centre too. They're in their truck on the road. Charlie points to Jog. 'Look!' he says. 'There's an alien in the car park!' 'No,' says Lily. 'That's Miss Kite in her new hat, I think. Yes, I think that's Miss Kite.' She opens the window and calls, 'Hello, Miss Kite!'

'Hello!' answers Jog. 'Shall I find a place for your truck here?'
'No, thanks!' Lily calls. Charlie and Lily aren't stopping. They're going to the cinema.
'Well, what about in the car park next to the station?' Jog asks.
'No,' Lily says. 'But thank you for asking, Miss Kite. Bye!'

Jog is outside the circus now. He likes watching the people there. The circus is opposite City Hospital.

Miss Kite and Miss Read live in Skiptown. They're going to the hospital today.

Miss Kite points to Jog. 'Look! There's an alien!' she says.

'Don't be silly!' says her friend. 'Put your glasses on! That's Mr Doors, I think. He's ill. Look! His face is green.'

'It isn't Mr Doors,' answers Miss Kite quietly. She knows Jog is an alien and she's afraid of aliens.

'Good afternoon!' says Jog. 'Shall I help you cross the road?'

'We're OK,' Miss Kite says.

'Well, shall I carry your bags for you?'

Aliens LOVE carrying bags.

'No!' she says. 'But thanks for asking! Goodbye!'

Jog is at the funfair in Skiptown now. There are lots of exciting rides at the funfair. One looks like a yellow spaceship!

Sam and his sister, Julia, live in Skiptown. They're riding in the yellow spaceship. Sam sees Jog and points to him.

'Look! An alien!' he says.

'Oh yes!' says Julia. 'Hi!'

Jog smiles. 'Good evening! My name's Jog!' he says.

Shall I take you for a ride above the town in MY spaceship?

'Wow! Yes please!' says Sam. 'And then, can you take us home?'

'Yes! No problem!' says Jog.

'What a kind alien! Thank you very much!' says Julia.

'I like helping people,' says Jog.

'And we like making friends with aliens!' say Sam and Julia.

2

Jog the alien

A Look, read and draw lines.

a cinema
a funfair
a circus
a supermarket
a playground
a hospital

B Put the sentences in order.

Ⓐ Jog has his picnic in the car park.   ☐

Ⓑ Jog wants to help two people cross the road.   ☐

Ⓒ Jog makes friends with two children.   ☐

Ⓓ Jog gets some food from a supermarket.   ☐ 1

Ⓔ Jog talks to two people in a truck.   ☐

C Answer the questions about Jog. Then answer for you.

❶ Which vegetables do aliens love eating?   o n i o n s

   What do you love eating?   ....

❷ What does Jog like counting?   c _ _ _

   What do you count at school?   ....

❸ Where are Charlie and Lily going to?   the c _ _ _ _ _

   Which places in town do you like going to?   ....

❹ What is Miss Kite afraid of?   a _ _ _ _ _

   Which animals are you afraid of?   ....

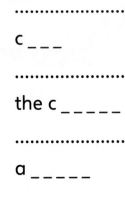

D Draw lines and then ask and answer.

1 Shall I help you wash your truck?

2 Shall we help you carry the shopping?

3 Shall I help you find your book?

4 Shall we help you feed the animals?

a Yes, please. Here! Take these bags.

b It's OK! Here it is! Look!

c Oh yes, please! It's really dirty.

d Not now, thanks. They aren't hungry!

E ▶ Where are the people in Mrs Doors' family? Listen and write a letter in each box.
05

Mr Doors `B`

A

Mrs Doors' sister

B

her son

C

her brother

D

her daughter

E

F Look and read. Choose the correct words and write.

a train

a bookshop

a playground

a bus

a motorbike

the town centre

1. There are a lot of shops in this place.   the town centre
2. Only one or two people can ride on this.   ....
3. You can buy story books in this place.   ....
4. This stops in the road and people get on it.   ....
5. Children come here to climb, run and have fun.   ....
6. This travels quickly to different stations.   ....

G Look, read and write.

Complete the sentences.

1. You can see two penguins on ....
2. Behind the station, there is ....

Answer the questions.

3. What is the woman wearing?   ....
4. Which animals can you see?   ....

Now write one sentence about the picture.

5. ....

H Look and write your shopping list. Then ask and answer.

Shall I get you some onions?

Shopping list

....
....
....
....
....
....
....
....

I ▶ Listen and circle the correct answer. Then sing the song.

06

The circus is in town today.
Come and see! Come and see!
I'm **sitting / going** here with
Tom and Sue
and my friend **Bill's / Fred's**
cool uncle too.

The circus is in town today!
Come and see! Come and see!
Clowns are **driving / washing** funny trains
and falling out of **scary / silly** planes.

The circus is in town today!
Come and see! Come and see!
We're **shouting / laughing** and
we're clapping hands
And **dancing / singing** with the
music man!

J Read and answer the questions.

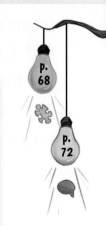

Do you live in a house or flat?

How do you go to your town?

Do you walk? Ride your bike? Go on a bus?

What do you like doing in your town?

Do you like going to the park? To the cinema?

Which is your favourite place in your town?

p. 68

p. 72

19

My friend Meg

Meg is my best friend. All our classmates like her because she's always happy and she's very funny. She can do long sums and spell long words. She can ride a bike very fast too.

But Meg is always losing things!
I can't do long sums.
I can't spell long words and I can't ride my bike very fast.
But I can always find Meg's things for her!
Meg phones me or I phone her every day.
It was Sunday yesterday.
Meg phoned me in the morning.
She was angry!

She said, 'I can't find my pencils. I need them for
maths tomorrow. I looked in my bag. I looked in our hall.
I looked on the table. I looked on our wall. I looked by the door,
then I looked on the floor. But ... I can't find my pencils.'
'Oh, Meg!' I said. 'Go and look under your bed!'
Meg loves reading comics and writing funny stories about all
kinds of people. She's good at drawing too. She likes drawing
funny clothes.

Meg likes wearing funny clothes and hats too. But she *doesn't* like
wearing shoes. She's always taking off her shoes! She loses her
shoes or her trainers every day because she puts them in lots of
different places!

Meg phoned me in the afternoon yesterday. She said, 'I can't find my trainers. I need them for our sports lesson tomorrow.
I looked in the cupboard,
then under the stairs.
I looked on the sofa
and under the chairs.
I looked in the box
and I looked by my socks.

But ... I can't find my trainers.'

'Oh, Meg!' I said. 'Go and look in your garden!'

Meg loves working on the computer because she likes finding out about things. She likes reading about different kinds of animals and about film stars and pop stars and music. She's really good at music. She has piano and guitar lessons. She has singing lessons at school too.

Meg always does her music homework, but then she loses it. She loses it because she puts books, comics or a board game on top of it!

Meg phoned me in the evening yesterday. She said,
'I can't find my homework. I need it for music tomorrow.
I looked on Dad's desk, then by his guitar.
I looked in Mum's bag and in the back of our car.
I looked in our kitchen and under the kitten.

But ... I can't find my homework.'

'Oh, Meg!' I said. 'Go and look by your laptop.'

It's Monday now. I'm putting my things in my school bag. I've got to run and catch the bus to school.

Meg phoned me *again* this morning! She said,
'Hey! I found my pencils! They *were* under my bed! Thanks!
I found my trainers! They *were* in the garden! Thank you!
I found my homework too! It *was* by my laptop!

Thanks for being my friend!

You're brilliant. You're really cool.
See you at the bus stop!'

3

My friend Meg

A Read and write the words.

1 Our little ......kitten...... loves eating fish and playing with its ball!

2 My favourite .... sings and plays the guitar.

3 Dad's working on his computer and Mum's working on her ....

4 This is my favourite .... Her new film is great.

B Read and say *right* or *wrong*!

1 Meg is a girl. — Right!

2 Meg loses lots of things.

3 Meg likes drawing funny clothes.

4 Meg can play the guitar.

5 Meg goes to school on a train.

6 Meg's things are always in the right places.

C When does Meg say these things? Draw lines.

1 I can't find my pencils!

2 I can't find my homework!

3 I need it for music.

4 I need them for maths.

5 I need them for sports.

6 I can't find my trainers!

in the morning

in the afternoon

in the evening

D Draw lines. Make sentences.

Thanks for being my friend!

1. Meg's friends like her because   her teacher wants it.
2. Meg's got lots of pencils because   she's happy and funny.
3. Meg wants her trainers because   she puts things on top of it.
4. Meg needs her homework because   she's got a sports lesson.
5. Meg loses her homework because   she enjoys drawing.

E Complete the sentences with a word from the box.

played listened watched painted ~~walked~~ cleaned

1. I .....walked..... to the park yesterday morning.
2. Meg .... the piano yesterday morning.
3. I .... a picture yesterday afternoon.
4. Meg .... her bike yesterday afternoon.
5. Meg and her mum .... to some music on Sunday.
6. Meg and her mum .... TV on Monday.

** Listen and colour and write.**
08

G **Read the text and choose the best answer.**

1   Meg: I can't find my school bag!

   Clare: Ⓐ It's under the tree!

          B No, it isn't.

          C I like school.

2   Meg: Can I read your new comic?

   Paul: **A** Don't worry!

          B Here you are!

          C Thank you.

3   Meg: What do you play in your music lesson?

   Alice: **A** Only the piano.

          B In the morning.

          C Every Sunday.

4   Meg: Thanks for being my friend, Hugo!

   Hugo: **A** I'd like that.

          B Well done!

          C That's OK!

H Look at the pictures. Write and tell the story.

Oh dear! Meg can't ....*find*........ her ....!
She looks in the .... and she looks in the ....
and then she looks behind the .... too!
She phones her friend and her friend says,

Go and look under your desk!

I Listen and write. Then write about your friend.
09

Name: ....*Clare*.............
Age: ....
This person is my friend because:
....

Colour of hair: ....
My friend likes: ....
My friend's favourite sport is: ....
My friend likes finding out about: ....

Name: ....
Age: ....
This person is my friend because:
....

Colour of hair: ....
My friend likes: ....
My friend's favourite sport is: ....
My friend likes finding out about: ....

 p. 69

p. 72

High five!

4

Tom and Zoe are listening to the radio. When their favourite band stops playing, a woman starts talking about a sports weekend at Treetop Park. 'Come and have a great weekend with Mr Hop and make lots of new friends,' the woman says. 'You can practise your favourite sports and try some new ones too!'

Come and play
on Saturday!
Baseball or soccer,
roller skating or basketball,
try skateboarding or dancing.
You can try it at Treetop Park!

Come and play
on Sunday!
Hockey or horse riding,
table tennis or badminton,
go ice skating or swimming.
You can do it at Treetop Park!

'I'd like to go!' says Tom.
'Me too!' says Zoe. 'Let's ask Dad.'
'OK,' Dad says. 'You're both good at sport but remember – you can't be good at EVERY sport!'

It's Saturday morning. Tom and Zoe are in Treetop Park and they're playing baseball.
'Watch Tom! He's great at baseball,' says Zoe to another girl, 'but I'm terrible at it. I can't catch balls!'
Tom hits the ball with his new bat. Zoe runs really quickly and falls on the ground.
'Ow! My arm!' she says. But then she smiles and shouts, 'But look! I've got the ball!'

The other children shout, 'Wow! Well done, Zoe!'
Tom's surprised. 'Yes!' he calls to Zoe. 'That was so cool!'
'Thanks, Tom!' Zoe answers. 'I AM good at baseball!' she thinks. 'And I CAN catch a ball. Fantastic!'
'Are you all right, Zoe?' Mr Hop asks.
'She's fine! Don't worry!' laughs Tom.

Now Tom and Zoe are playing soccer. 'Watch Zoe! She's great at soccer!' Tom says to another boy, 'but I'm not. I'm not good at kicking footballs.'

Everyone's enjoying the game. Zoe kicks the ball to Tom and shouts, 'Let's get another goal now, Tom. You try! You can do it!'

Tom laughs and kicks the ball, but falls on the ground.

'Ow! My leg!' he says. 'But, look! The ball's in the net!'

The other children jump up and down and clap loudly.

'Goal! Well done, Tom!' they shout.

Zoe's very happy. 'Yes! That was really great, Tom!' she calls.

'Cool!' Tom says. 'Wow,' he thinks. 'I AM good at soccer. I CAN score goals! Fantastic!'

'Are you OK, Tom?' Mr Hop asks.

'He's fine! Don't worry!' laughs Zoe.

High five!

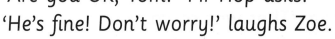

'Good!' Mr Hop says. 'What next? There's roller skating, basketball, skateboarding and dancing.'
'Brilliant!' Tom says to Zoe. 'I want to try rollerskating and basketball.'
'What about skateboarding and dancing?' asks Zoe.
'Well, I'm not good at those … But, yes!' answers Tom.
'Me too!' laughs Zoe.
'OK!' Mr Hop answers. 'Come on!'

Tom and Zoe go home at the end of the afternoon. When their father sees them, he laughs and says, 'Well, I was right. You can't be good at every sport! Are you OK?'

'We're fine, Dad. Don't worry!' Zoe says. 'We've got lots of new friends and we had lots of fun. Oh! And Tom is a brilliant soccer player!'
'And Zoe is great at baseball!' says Tom. 'Can we go and play with our ball before dinner?'

High five!

4

A — Look, read and complete the words.

1. Look at me! I'm ꞁ o ꞁ ꞁ er skating! Come and try it too!
2. I like _a _ _ i _ _ with my friends. Do you?
3. I didn't know that! I'm very su _ _ _ _ _ ed!
4. Kick the ball into the _e_! Goal! Well done!
5. This music is by my favourite _ a _ _. They're great!
6. Here's my new _ _a _ e _ oa _ _. Do you like it?

B — Read and answer the questions.

1. What is the name of Zoe's brother? ....Tom.........
2. Which day do the children go to Treetop Park? ....
3. Who is the children's sports teacher? ....
4. Which sport is Zoe playing when she catches a ball? ....
5. What does Tom hurt when he scores a goal? his ....
6. Zoe says Tom is very good at which sport? ....

C — Look at the pictures. Tell the story.

Zoe's playing baseball.

High five!

D Draw lines. Make sentences.

1 Zoe starts dancing   a hockey but loves playing badminton.

2 Tom loves ice   b go swimming in the lake.

3 Zoe's friends don't   c that ball, Tom. Throw it to me.

4 Please stop kicking   d skating with his friends on Saturdays.

5 Mr Hop doesn't play   e when the band plays her favourite song.

E Read about table tennis. Choose the right words.

Table tennis

1 Two or more people ....can........ play table tennis. You need a ball   **can**   shall   would

2 .... a table with a net for this game. You need a bat, too.   but   because   and

3 Some people call .... bats 'rackets'. You hit the ball   they   them   their

4 .... your bat. It can only bounce once! Then your friend hits it back to you. The game ends when   from   with   for

5 .... person scores 11 points.   one   an   both

6 When you start .... table tennis, it's difficult! But practise and practise! It's a great sport!   play   playing   plays

11 ▶ Where are Tom's sports things? Listen and write a letter in each box.

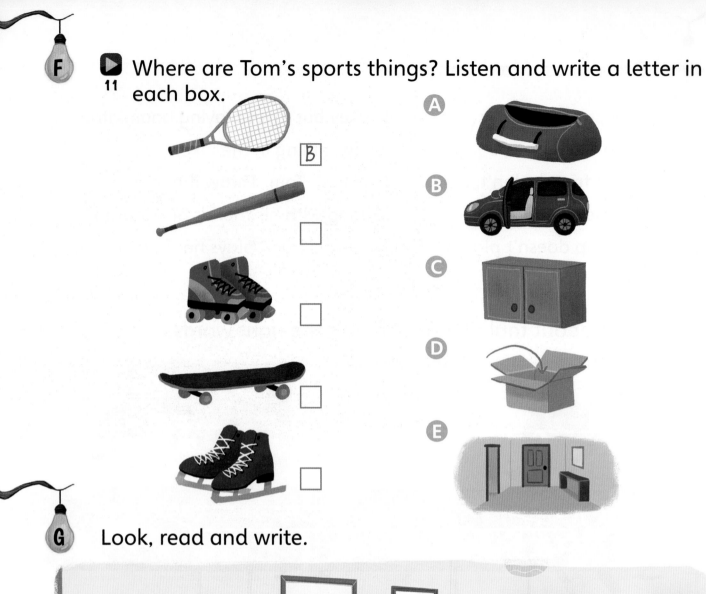

Complete the sentences.

1 The children are at home in ....

2 Their father is holding ....

Answer the questions.

3 What kind of food is on the plate? ....

4 Where is the sports bag? ....

Now write one sentence about the picture.

5 ....

G Look, read and write.

H Which one is different? Circle and say.

> The baseball cap! You wear a baseball cap but you don't wear your nose, ears and mouth!

I ▶ **12** Listen and tick (✔) the sports you hear.

skateboarding	✔	hockey	☐	horse riding	☐
fishing	☐	tennis	☐	basketball	☐
ice skating	☐	football	☐	swimming	☐

J Think of six sentences. Then mime and ask *What am I doing?*

bounce walk fall stop start
hit hurt
throw run skip hop watch jump
swim drop hold catch climb dance play
ride carry move

> You're holding a book!

> You're bouncing a ball!

> Your leg is hurting!

p. 69

p. 72

The monster under my bed!

There's a monster upstairs. It's living in my bedroom this week. It's under my bed.

When I get up in the morning, I have to run to my cupboard very quickly. I take out my clothes and then run to the bathroom. I put my clothes on in there. I don't want to get dressed in my bedroom. I don't want the monster to come out from under my bed and take my socks or my favourite sweater.

After school, I don't play computer games. My computer is on the desk in my bedroom. I don't want to sit there with my feet on the floor. When I'm not looking, the monster comes out. I think it wants to eat my toes!

And I can't do my homework in my bedroom. I think the monster
wants to write or draw on all the pages in my school books.
I'm doing all my homework on the kitchen table this week.
Mum says that's OK.

When I want to go to bed, I open the door to my bedroom
and say very loudly, 'I know you're in here but this is my room!
You aren't scary!' The monster listens, I think. It doesn't come out.
I never see it. But it is scary. I know it's there.

I quickly run and jump into bed and then close my eyes and count to
100. 'Counting helps you to go to sleep,' Grandma says.
When you're counting to 100, you don't think about monsters.

When I'm asleep at night, I think
the monster climbs quietly out of
my window. I think it finds things
to eat in our garden. I know it
comes back again before morning.

I told my brother about the monster. He laughed and said, 'Don't be silly, Vicky! There are no monsters under your bed, but there's a very big one under mine. There's one in my cupboard too.' I think my brother likes monsters. He draws lots of pictures of them and puts them on his walls.

I told Mum about the monster. She laughed and said, 'I didn't see any monsters under your bed when I cleaned your room yesterday.' I think the monster hides when she goes in my room. This monster is a very, very clever one!

I told Dad about the monster. He said, 'Don't worry! I'm not afraid of monsters. We can find it and tell it to go away.' But Dad didn't come and help me when I asked him to. He wanted to watch a film on television with Uncle Bill. I think Dad IS scared of monsters. I can understand that.

It's Saturday today. My brother and my parents don't want to help me, but I don't want to live with this scary monster for another week. I want to play computer games in my bedroom again.

I'm going upstairs now. I want to find the monster and tell it to go away. It can go and live with Mrs Gray. She lives in the house next to ours. My brother and I don't like her!

So, I'm looking under my bed ... I know there's a monster here. I think it's got lots of legs and a big round stomach and big scary teeth. I think it's got huge black eyes ...

But I can't see it. And I can't hear it.

Oh yes, I can. There it is!

I can do this!

Slowly ... quietly ... slowly ... quietly ... *Got you!!!*

5

The monster under my bed!

A Read and write the words.

hide ~~laugh~~ climb **get dressed** help

1. You do this when something is very funny. ......*laugh*.......

2. This means 'put on clothes'. ....

3. You do this when you want to go up something like a tree. ....

4. Do this when you don't want anyone to see you. ....

5. When you can't do something, ask someone to do this. ....

B Read and circle the correct answer.

1. The monster is in Vicky's **bathroom** / (**bedroom**)

2. The monster hides under a **cupboard** / **bed**.

3. Vicky counts to **100** / **200** when she goes to bed.

4. The monster **cleans** / **climbs** out of Vicky's room at night.

5. Vicky's brother has lots of **books** / **pictures** about monsters.

6. **Vicky's dad** / **Vicky** finds the monster at the end of the story.

C Who's talking about the story? Tick (✔) the correct box.

This is about a huge monster. It takes some socks and hides them under a girl's bed. It's scary but I laughed a lot at the end of the story. ☐

This story is about a girl and a spider. She thinks it's a monster! She's frightened of the monster but she's brave too. I liked the picture of her room at night. ☐

D Complete the sentences. Write one word.

1 The monster lives ....upstairs.... in Vicky's bedroom.

2 Vicky's .... are in her cupboard.

3 There's a .... on Vicky's desk.

4 Vicky doesn't want to put her .... on the floor.

5 Vicky does her .... downstairs in the kitchen.

6 The .... under her brother's bed is huge.

E Write *I think...* or *I know...*

1 .....I think..... the monster goes into the garden at night.

2 .... I've got ten toes.

3 .... monsters and aliens live on the moon.

4 .... monsters are really scary in some stories.

5 .... the word **monster** has got seven letters in it.

F Look at the picture on page 37. Find six differences.

▶ **14** Write the colours. Then look at page 38. Listen, colour and write.

b.lack.......... w................ b................. g.................

b................ p................ g................. o.................

p................ y................ r................

H Complete the sentences with a word from the box.

Lily   Mark

Mary   Bill   Jack   Jill

Peter   Vicky

| sister | ~~brother~~ | son | aunt | grandparents | parents |

1. My .....brother..... is called Peter.
2. My .... are called Jack and Jill.
3. Mary and Bill are my .... and uncle.
4. My .... are called Lily and Mark.
5. Aunt Mary is my dad's ....
6. Peter is my mother's ....

I Draw lines. Make sentences.

1. My aunt gave me a drink **when**
2. My brother drew a monster **when**
3. My uncle bought me two e-books **when**
4. My cousins went swimming **when**
5. My parents cleaned the kitchen **when**

he got some new pencils.

they went to the beach.

I was thirsty.

it was dirty.

it was my birthday.

J Listen and write about Vicky's brother.

15

1. Name: ....Peter........
2. Age: ....
3. Favourite hobby: ....
4. Doesn't like: ....
5. Favourite colour: ....
6. Number of comics on the floor of his room: ....

K Read the sentences and tell the story. It is called 'Don't worry!'

Help! There's a monster under my bed!

Mum:
Don't worry! You can do your homework in the kitchen.

Grandma:
Don't worry! Count to 100. That helps me go to sleep.

Dad:
Don't worry! I'm not afraid of monsters. I can come and help you.

Peter:
Don't worry! Monsters are really cool!

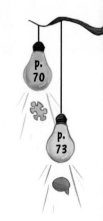

p. 70

p. 73

What a great grandmother!

6

Peter's grandmother is 71, and every day she does the same things at the same time. She always gets up at seven o'clock.
She always gets dressed at eight o'clock. She always has breakfast (two pieces of bread, a banana and a cup of tea) at nine o'clock.

She always listens to music on the radio at ten. It's her favourite part of the day.
She always has a cup of coffee at 11 and then she goes for a short walk before lunch (down to the square, round the park and back home again) and she always has her lunch (fish, chips and peas with tomato sauce) at 12 o'clock.

On Friday afternoons, Peter often goes to see his grandmother.
Last week, he slept at her house on Friday night too.
On Saturday morning, he got up at seven o'clock and ran
downstairs to talk to her.

'I've got an idea, Gran!' Peter said. 'Let's have a crazy day!'

'What do you mean?' she asked.

'Well ... you always do the same things at the same time every day.'

'Yes ... ?'

'Well, today, let's have a different day. I'm hungry! Let's have our
breakfast now. And let's have egg sandwiches or sausages!'

'But I never have egg sandwiches or sausages for breakfast, Peter!' his
grandmother said. But then she looked at Peter's face and said, 'OK!'

'Those sausages were really good!' Peter's grandmother said after
breakfast. 'I liked them a lot!'
'I enjoyed them too,' Peter said. 'Right, now let's get dressed.
Then let's go for a walk.'

'But I always listen to the radio first ...' his grandmother started to
say. But then she stopped. 'All right! Good idea! Where's my coat?'

Peter's grandmother enjoyed their walk but when they got to the square, Peter said, 'Let's catch a bus to Market Street.
There's a really cool café between the library and the shopping centre. We can look at the shops and then have our lunch there too!'

'But I never catch buses, Peter, and I never go to the shopping centre in Market Street and I never eat in cafés!' Peter's grandmother said.
But then she looked at the smile on Peter's face and said, 'OK! Come on

Peter's grandmother enjoyed walking around the shopping centre. She bought a new watch, a fantastic purple and yellow sweater and a little cupboard for her bathroom. Then, in another shop, she found an exciting board game for Peter.

'I'm having lots of fun!' she said. 'What a great day!'

When they got to the café, Peter said, 'Let's have noodles!'

Let's have pancakes too! Chocolate ones!

'But I never have noodles or pancakes!' Peter's grandmother said. But then she smiled and said, 'All right! I can try them, today.'

After lunch, Peter's grandmother said, 'Everything was brilliant! Those noodles and chocolate pancakes were fantastic. I loved them!'

'Good!' Peter said. 'Now let's go home. I know you sometimes sleep in the afternoon ... and I'm tired!'

'But I don't want to go home and I don't want to sleep this afternoon, Peter,' his grandmother said.

'Let's go for a boat ride on the river and then go for a walk all around the lake. We can buy cakes and eat them in the park and then we can go to the cinema! I never do any of those things but I'd like to do them all today!'

Peter smiled. 'OK, Gran!' he said. 'Let's go! You know, you really are a great grandmother!'

'And you really are a great grandson, Peter!' she laughed.

6 What a great grandmother!

A Look, read and write the word.

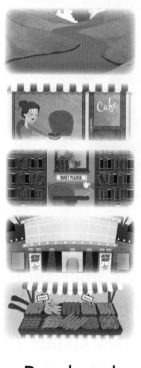

1 It's fun to go for a boat ride along this. a ....river.......

2 You can sit and buy something to eat here. a ....

3 People come here to look at books. a ....

4 This is where you go to watch films. a ....

5 This is outside. People go shopping here. a ....

B Read and answer the questions.

1 How old is Peter's grandmother? ....71.........

2 When does she always get up in the morning? ....

3 What does she always listen to in the morning? ....

4 Which day does Peter go to Market Street? ....

5 Where does Gran want to eat cakes? ....

C What did Gran eat? How did she travel? Where did she go to? Circle the words.

Trying new things is fun!

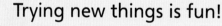

noodles   pie   (sausages)   pancakes   burgers
bus   train   plane   bike   boat   cinema
zoo   shopping centre   café   supermarket

D Complete the sentences. Write 1, 2 or 3 words.

1. Peter slept at his grandmother's house last ....Friday........ night.
2. Peter's grandmother gets dressed at .... o'clock.
3. .... has a banana and bread for breakfast.
4. She has a .... at 11 o'clock.
5. She walks to the .... and the park every morning.
6. At 12 o'clock, she has fish, ... with tomato sauce.

E Circle *always*, *often*, *sometimes* and *never* in these sentences.

> 'I always have bread and a banana for breakfast!'
>
> On Friday afternoons, Peter often goes to see his grandmother.
>
> 'Now let's go home. I know you sometimes sleep in the afternoon.'
>
> 'But I never have sausages for breakfast, Peter!'

Complete the sentences with *always*, *often*, *sometimes* or *never*.

1. I .... get up at seven o'clock.
2. I .... listen to music in the evening.
3. I .... drink coffee.
4. I .... eat pancakes for lunch.

F Look at the picture on page 45. Find six differences.

G Read the text and choose the best answer.

1 Peter: Let's have sausages!

Gran: **(A)** All right!

 B Me too!

 C Goodbye!

2 Peter: Where's the bus stop?

Gran: **A** At 11 o'clock.

 B No, I never go there.

 C At the end of the road.

3 Peter: When do you get dressed?

Gran: **A** A pink dress, I think.

 B Before breakfast.

 C What a good idea!

4 Peter: Would you like to sit down?

Gran: **A** No, I'm fine!

 B Oh dear!

 C Well done!

H Read and write the words.

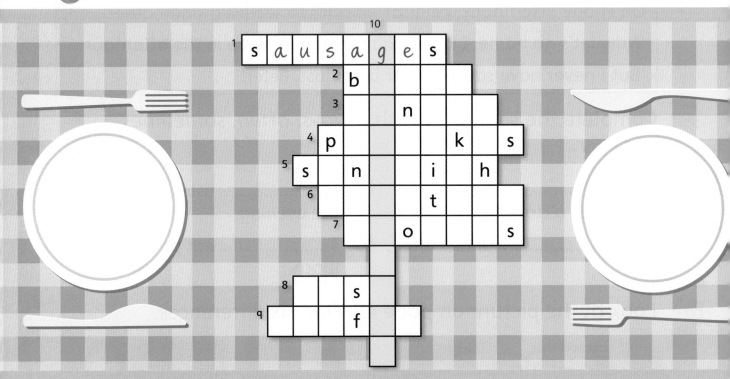

1 Grandmother has these for breakfast with Peter. They are meat.

2 Grandmother always eats some of this for breakfast.

3 This fruit is long and yellow.

4 Grandmother has these in the café with chocolate!

5 You can make this with bread and cheese.

6 These are round and red.

7 These are long and thin. Grandmother has these in the café too.

8 This is Grandmother's favourite food for lunch.

9 Grandmother drinks this every day at 11 o'clock.

I Choose new words for the green words. Write a different story!

'Let's go for a boat ride **1** on the river and then go for a walk **2** all around the lake. We can buy **3** cakes and eat them **4** in the park and then we can **5** go to the cinema. I never do any of those things but I'd like to do them all today!' Peter's **6** grandmother said.

1 ...at the beach...   **2** ....   **3** ....
4 ....   **5** ....   **6** ....

J Complete the text about your day in town.

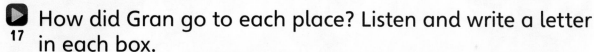

After .... , I want to go to town with my ....
We can go to town by .... First, we can go to the
.... I'd like to buy .... After that, we can eat some
.... Then I'd like to ....

K ▶ **How did Gran go to each place? Listen and write a letter in each box.**
17

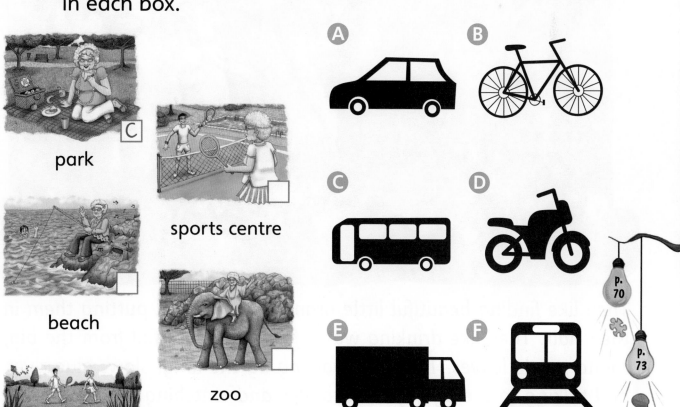

park   C

sports centre

beach

zoo

river

p. 70

p. 73

The old man and the jungle

7

The old man and the child live in the jungle. The jungle is their home. They like listening to the tall banana trees when they move in the wind. They like listening to the blue parrots and the noises of all the other jungle animals and birds. They like growing vegetables in the old man's jungle garden and making and eating sweet jungle fruit cake.

They like finding beautiful little orange flowers and putting them in their hair. They like drinking water from the waterfall from the big, round jungle leaves. They like walking by the long, slow, blue river and talking to the ugly, fat crocodiles and watching the small, yellow fish swim here and there, here and there, in the water.

And they both love sitting quietly in the sun.

But one day in the jungle, there was no sun in the big jungle sky. The old man wasn't happy about that. He sat in his old chair and didn't move. The child came and sat down on the green grass next to him.

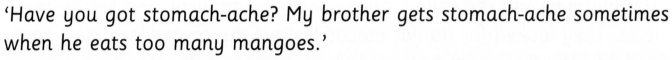

What's the matter, Old man?

'Have you got stomach-ache? My brother gets stomach-ache sometimes when he eats too many mangoes.'

'A stomach-ache? Oh, no! My stomach is fine, thank you,' answered the old man.

'Well, have you got an earache?' the child asked. 'My mother gets earache sometimes when I play my jungle drums too loudly.'

'An earache? Oh, no! My ears are fine, thank you,' answered the old man.

The old man and the child stopped talking and went and sat in the tree. They listened for the parrots and the noises of the other jungle animals and birds but the parrots didn't come.

'Well, have you got a toothache?' asked the child. 'My cousins get toothache sometimes when they drink too much lime juice.'

'Toothache? Oh, no! My teeth are fine, thank you,' answered the old man.

'Have you got a headache, then?'

'No.'

'A temperature? A cold? A cough?'

'No.'

The old man and the child stopped talking and went and sat by the river. They looked for the fat crocodiles but the crocodiles didn't come and no little fish swam here and there, here and there.

Then the beautiful sun came out and the old man smiled.

'Are you getting better now?' the child asked.

'Yes,' said the old man.

They saw their favourite crocodile's head above the water and three little fish came and started swimming here and there, here and there, again.

Then the old man's favourite parrot flew down from the waterfall and sat on his shoulder and said, 'Getting better, getting better?'
'Yes, clever parrot,' said the old man. 'I'm better now, thank you.'
And the child and the old man laughed loudly.
'I'm very well again now.' he said. 'I'm very, very well.'
'Good' said the child.
They walked home, watered the vegetables and danced in the old man's garden under the sun. Then the old man and the child made the best sweet fruit cake in the jungle and ate it all ...

'Ate it all? Ate it all?' the parrot said.
'Be careful, Old Man!
Too much cake! Stomach-ache!'

7 The old man and the jungle

A Look at the pictures and find the words.

headacheearachecoughtoothachecoldstomachache

B Put the sentences in order.

- Ⓐ The child and the old man sat in a tree. ☐
- Ⓑ The parrot sat on the old man's shoulder. ☐
- Ⓒ There was no sun in the sky. ☐
- Ⓓ The child and the old man looked for the crocodiles. 1
- Ⓔ The child asked about earache. ☐
- Ⓕ The child and the old man made a fruit cake. ☐
- Ⓖ The child sat down on some grass. ☐

C Read and complete the words.

1. They drink the water from the w a t e r f a l l.
2. The old man grows v _ _ _ _ _ _ _ _ _ in his garden.
3. The leaves in the jungle are r _ _ _ _ and green.
4. The old man thinks the parrot is c _ _ _ _ _ .
5. The child sometimes plays d _ _ _ _ very loudly.
6. When the old man s _ _ _ _ _ , he looks happy.

D Ask and answer with a friend.

E Read the text. Complete the sentences. Write 1, 2 or 3 words.

They like finding beautiful little orange flowers and putting them in their hair. They like drinking water from the waterfall from the big, round jungle leaves. They like walking by the long, slow, blue river and talking to the ugly, fat crocodiles and watching the small, yellow fish swim here and there, here and there, in the water.

1 The child sometimes puts small ..*orange flowers*.. in his hair.

2 The jungle leaves they drink their water from are big and
....

3 The old man and the child go for walks next to the
.... river.

4 The crocodiles in this story are ugly and ....

5 Some small .... swim in the water.

F Read about jungles. Choose the right words.

Jungles

① Trees are always green ....*in*.......... the	on	in	at
② jungle. Some jungles are	call	calls	called
③ 'rainforests'. Lots of animals	live	living	lives
there. You can sometimes find huge			
frogs in jungles. Some jungle frogs can			
④ ....! Many people think jungle	fly	flying	flies
⑤ snakes .... spiders are scary.	but	and	because
Lots of children enjoy reading stories			
⑥ .... jungles. Do you?	about	to	under

G ▶ Listen and say. Circle the words that sound the same.
19

Quietly, quietly!

We're going on a jungle walk.

Shh! Don't talk!

We're going on a jungle walk at night …

Are you all right?

We're going on a jungle walk at night… Look! Bats!

Put on your hats!

Scary! Scary!

Let's go home!

H Which one is different? Circle and say.

①

②  

③

I  Listen and draw lines.

20

Anna   Paul   Lucy

Matt   Grace   Charlie

J   Complete your story.

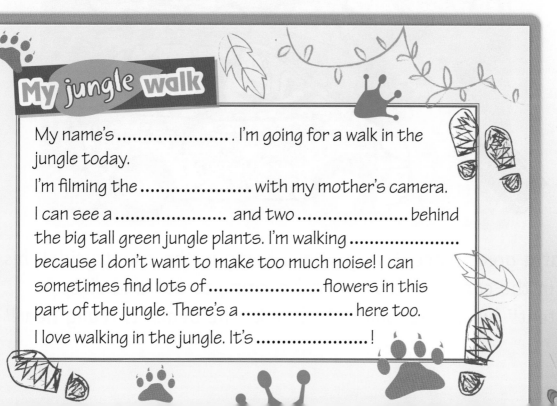

My jungle walk

My name's .... I'm going for a walk in the jungle today.

I'm filming the .... with my mother's camera.

I can see a .... and two .... behind the big tall green jungle plants. I'm walking .... because I don't want to make too much noise! I can sometimes find lots of .... flowers in this part of the jungle. There's a .... here too.

I love walking in the jungle. It's ....!

p. 71

p. 73

Henry's holiday

Henry likes being at home in the school holidays. He likes looking for lizards and snails and flying his kite in the field behind his house. He likes listening to music and watching television. He likes playing games on his tablet and reading comics in bed. He likes getting up in the night and eating ice cream in the kitchen too.

Henry doesn't enjoy going on holiday to different places. He doesn't want to get sand in his socks on the beach or go for long walks in the countryside and he doesn't want to sleep in a room with his parents because his dad SNORES!

But last Saturday, Henry and his parents went on holiday.

'What a great place, Henry. I love being in the countryside!' his father said in the car. 'And it's fun and exciting to eat and sleep in a tent!' his mother said. 'And look! The beach is really near!'

'Sand in my socks and sharks in the sea. Oh dear!' thought Henry. Then he saw the hills. 'Oh no! Boring long walks!' he thought. 'And there's no games room and no TV. I want to go home!'

Henry's parents started to take the tent, their clothes, their holiday chairs and table out of the car.
'Can you come and help us, Henry?' they called. 'We've got to put up the tent now!' But Henry didn't move.
'The weather's terrible, Mum!' he called. 'It's cold and windy!'
'OK,' she said.

Then it started to rain. 'Please snow too!' Henry thought.
'I want to go home!'

Henry's mother took their sleeping things out of the car, but she dropped two of the blankets on the ground and they got very wet. 'Oh dear!' she said.

Henry got out of the car. He picked up the wet blankets and gave them to his mother. 'Can we go home now, Mum?' he asked.

But they didn't go home. Henry, his mum and dad sat in the tent. They didn't read. (Dad didn't bring their glasses or their new torches.) They only had cold soup for dinner. (The bread and Henry's favourite cheese weren't in the car! They were on the kitchen table at home.)

Henry tried to sleep but his head and shoulders got cold and he woke up 42 times in the night because his dad snored and snored and snored and snored!

In the morning, Henry's dad had a bad headache. His mum's back hurt. The water in the showers was cold (brrrrrrrrrr!) and the little village shop was closed on Sundays too. Oh! And Henry found a lizard in his shoe!

Henry's parents weren't happy. Henry wasn't happy.

'I know!'

'Mum ... Dad ...,' Henry said slowly. 'Can we have a holiday at home? 'We can have hot showers in the mornings. We can go for walks and look for snails in our field in the afternoons. We can have nice hot dinners in the evenings. Then we can watch funny films on TV and then you can go to sleep in your bed and I can go to sleep in mine.'

Henry's mum looked at Henry's dad and then they both looked at Henry again.

'Yes! Great idea!' they said. 'Come on! Let's put all these wet things in the car and go home!'

8

Henry's holiday

A Read and complete the words.

① Some people have one of these on their bed.   a b l a n k e t

② This small animal has a shell on its back.   a s n _ _ l

③ This has funny pictures and stories in it.   a c _ _ _ c

④ These are between your neck and your arms.   s _ _ u l _ e _ s

⑤ You stand in this to wash your body.   a s _ _ w _ r

⑥ This is hot and you eat it from a bowl.   s _ u _

B Read and circle the correct answer.

① Henry **likes** / (**doesn't like**) going on holiday.

② Henry's family went on a holiday in the **countryside** / **mountains**.

③ They came home again last **Saturday** / **Sunday**.

④ Henry slept very **well** / **badly** in the tent that night.

⑤ There was a **spider** / **lizard** in Henry's shoe in the morning.

C Look at the pictures. Tell the story with words from the box.

Henry is reading.

driving eating reading sleeping tent bed
car soup morning afternoon evening night

D Draw lines to the correct box.

eating ice cream

listening to music

watching television

having hot showers

😊 Henry likes	Henry doesn't like 🙁

going on holiday

finding snails

having sand in his socks

going for long walks

having hot dinners

sleeping in a tent

reading comics

E Read and write.

Oh no! It's raining! I don't want to get wet.

I know! I can put on a hat and coat and I can run to school!

1 I walked home in the snow and now I'm really cold!

2 I'm hungry but I haven't got any food in my school bag.

3 I'm tired after a long walk.

4 I'm ill and I've got a temperature.

65

F   ▶ Listen and tick (✔) the box.
22

1 What didn't Dad take on holiday?

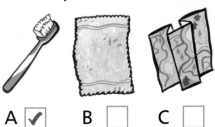

A ✔   B ☐   C ☐

2 What is in Mum's bag?

A ☐   B ☐   C ☐

3 Where is Henry's kite now?

A ☐   B ☐   C ☐

4 What is for breakfast?

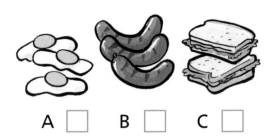

A ☐   B ☐   C ☐

G Complete the sentences. Write 1 or 2 words.

1 Henry's family went on holiday last ...Saturday... .

2 Henry can't play on his .... or watch TV on holiday.

3 .... didn't get out of the car because it was cold and windy.

4 Henry .... up lots of times in the night.

5 In the morning, Henry's dad had a ....

6 There was a .... in one of Henry's shoes.

H Look at the picture on page 63. Find eight differences.

I Read and complete the story. Choose a word from the box.

spiders   rained   shoe   ~~sunny~~   crocodile   sleeping   legs

Last Wednesday, it was very ① ......sunny...... and I found a lizard in our garden. Lizards like eating flies and ② .... too! My teacher told me that. I drew a picture of the lizard. It had a very long green tail and four short ③ .... When I showed my picture to Mum, she said, 'It looks like a baby ④ ....!'
That night, it ⑤ .... 'Oh no!' I said. 'Lizards don't like getting wet!' 'Don't worry!' Dad said. 'Lizards like ⑥ .... under rocks.' 'Great!' I said. 'There are lots of those by the flowers in our garden!'

J Read and write the days under the correct pictures.

Friday	**Sunday**
It rained and rained today. I got very wet when I walked into town.	There was a beautiful rainbow in the sky today but I didn't have my camera.
Saturday	**Monday**
Today it was very cold but I didn't watch TV. I had lots of fun outside in the park.	The weather was great but I didn't fly my kite today. I went for a walk and I had an ice cream.

p 73

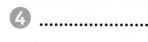

① .... ② .... ③ .... ④ ....

Let's have fun!

1 Find out more about an animal. Make a poster.

It lives …

This is my animal. It's a …

2 Draw some shops in a street where you live.
What can you buy? Write a list.

Shopping list
_____
_____
_____
_____
_____
_____
_____
_____

3 What is a good friend? Do a survey. Ask your classmates.

> Good friends are funny. Yes or no?

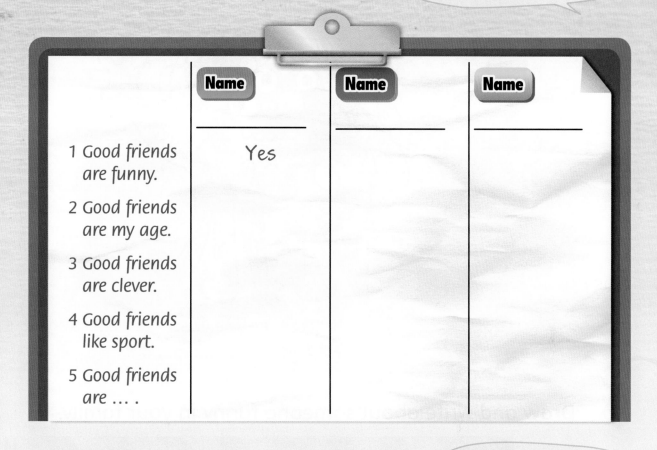

	Name	Name	Name
1 Good friends are funny.	Yes		
2 Good friends are my age.			
3 Good friends are clever.			
4 Good friends like sport.			
5 Good friends are			

4 Make a poster and tell your classmates.

> This sport is tennis. You need a tennis racket and a ball.

tennis racket

balls

Tennis

5 Draw and write about a monster.

My monster lives in ....

It likes eating .... and it's very good at ....

6 Draw and write about someone funny in your family.

This is my grandfather.
His name is _____.
He's wearing _____.
_____
_____

7 Colour the map and write about three animals that live there.

Parrots	....	....
Parrots live in the rainforest in South America. They are clever birds. Some parrots can talk.		

8 Do a weather project for this week. Make a poster.

Days of the week	Weather	Temperature
Monday	sunny	35°C
Tuesday		
Wednesday		
Thursday		
Friday		
Saturday		
Sunday		

Let's speak!

1 Play the game. Say more animals.

I'm learning about monkeys.

I'm learning about monkeys and tigers.

2 Imagine that you're telling Jog about your town.

Jog, this is my town. Here is the bookshop.

3 Talk about things you are good at.

I'm good at drawing! You're good at writing funny stories.

Thank you!

4 Imagine that you're making friends with Zoe.

Hello, I'm .... What's your name?

Hi, I'm Zoe.

5 Draw your family tree. Tell your partner.

My grandmother's name is Katia.

Have you got any cousins?

6 Talk about your day. Ask and answer.

What do you do before breakfast?

I get dressed.

7 What's the matter? Ask and answer.

Have you got earache?

Yes, I have.

8 What do you like doing on holiday? Ask and answer.

I like listening to music.

I like reading comics.

Let's say!

▶ ① 23

Jack and the zebra are skateboarding and swimming at the zoo.

▶ ② 24

Jog and Sam are in the cinema with a monkey.

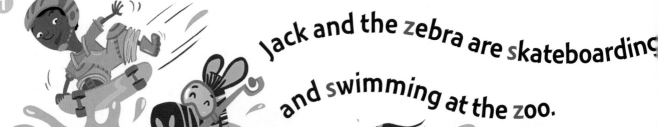

HAHAHA!

▶ ③ 25

Meg really likes roller skating and running in long races with Lucy.

▶ ④ 26

Tom's friends like to play baseball with their favourite vegetables.

▶ **5**
27

Vicky and her grandma enjoy jumping games with Jane's jellyfish.

▶ **6**
28

Peter and his grandmother had a milkshake and chocolate chips in the shopping centre.

▶ **7**
29

The old man and the fat crocodiles play jungle drums under the sun.

▶ **8**
30

Henry's little kitchen is full of cheese and bees.

Wordlist

1 Jack and the penguins

nouns
afternoon
animal
baby
bat
bird
bowl
boy
burger
cat
cheese
cupboard
dad
day
dog
dolphin
donkey
drink
ear
elephant
father
fish
fly
food
frog
fruit juice
giraffe
grape
Jack
kangaroo
kitchen

kiwi
leg
lemonade
meat
milk
milkshake
monkey
morning
mother
night
park
penguin
pet
phone
photo
pie
potato
sandwich
shark
snail
son
spider
story
today
twenty
water
waterfall
watermelon
whale
zebra
zoo
adjectives
big

blue
favourite
grey
hungry
little
sad
thirsty
wrong
verbs
answer
ask
bring
come
eat
enjoy
feed
fly
get
go
help
jump
know
laugh
learn
like
look
love
pick up
put
smile
take
want
wash

work
adverbs
again
carefully
down
up
expressions
how many
how much
great
please
sorry
wow

2 Jog the alien

nouns
alien
bag
bean
Bill
bird
bike
book
bookshop
bus
car
car park
centre
Charlie
children
cinema
circus
city

clothes
clown
door
driver
face
Fred
friend
funfair
glasses
hand
hat
home
hospital
Jog
Julia
kite
Lily
man
Miss
Mr
Mrs
music
name
onion
people
picnic
place
plane
playground
ride
road
Sam
school
shopping
sister
spaceship
station
street
Sue
supermarket

Tom
town
train
tree
truck
uncle
vegetable
window

adjectives
afraid
cool
dirty
exciting
funny
green
ill
new
scary
silly
top
yellow

verbs
buy
call
carry
clap
count
cross
dance
drive
fall
live
make
open
point
read
ride
say
see
shout

sing
sit
stop
wave
wear

adverbs
now
quietly
really

expressions
bye
good evening
good morning
goodbye
thanks

③ My friend Meg

nouns
age
Alice
bed
board game
box
chair
Clare
classmate
comic
computer
desk
door
film
floor
garden
girl
guitar
hall
homework
Hugo
kitten
laptop

lesson
maths
Meg
Monday
mum
Paul
pencil
piano
picture
pop star
shoe
sock
sofa
sport
stairs
sum
Sunday
table
teacher
thing
tomorrow
trainers
TV
wall
woman
word
yesterday

adjectives
angry
best
brilliant
clever
different
easy
great
happy
long

verbs
catch
clean

do
draw
listen
lose
need
paint
phone
play
run
spell
walk
write
adverbs
always
fast
expressions
good at
hey
well done

4 High five!

nouns
arm
badminton
ball
band
baseball
baseball cap
basketball
bat
brother
dancing
dinner
everyone
football
fun
goal
ground
hockey
home

hop
horse riding
ice skating
lake
mouth
net
nose
player
point
racket
radio
roller skating
Saturday
skateboarding
soccer
song
Sunday
swimming
table tennis
Tom
weekend
Zoe
adjectives
brilliant
difficult
fantastic
fine
surprised
terrible
verbs
bounce
climb
drop
hit
hold
hurt
kick
move
practise
remember

skip
start
try
adverbs
loudly
quickly
expressions
don't worry
high five!

5 The monster under the bed!

nouns
aunt
bathroom
beach
bedroom
Bill
birthday
computer
  game
cousin
daughter
e-book
eye
feet
grandma
grandparent
hobby
letter
monster
moon
night
page
parent
room
stomach
sweater
teeth
television

toe
uncle
Vicky
week
adjectives
asleep
black
brave
brown
frightened
gray
green
huge
orange
pink
purple
red
round
scared
white
verbs
close
draw
get dressed
hear
hide
sleep
take out
understand
adverbs
downstairs
never
slowly
upstairs

6 What a great grandmother!

nouns
banana
boat

bread
breakfast
bus stop
café
cake
chip
chocolate
coat
coffee
cup
dress
egg
Friday
grandmother
grandson
idea
library
lunch
market
noodle
o'clock
pancake
part
pea
Peter
piece
plane
river
sandwich
sauce
sausage
shop
shopping
  centre
square
tea
ten
time
tomato
train

adjectives
crazy
last
little
long
same
short
thin
tired
verbs
mean
adverbs
often
sometimes

7 The old man and the jungle

nouns
child
cold
cough
crocodile
drum
earache
flower
fruit
grass
hair
juice
jungle
leaves
lime
mango
mother
noise
parrot
rainforest
shoulder
sky
snake

stomach-ache
sun
temperature
toothache
water
wind
adjectives
beautiful
better
careful
cold
fat
ill
long
old
slow
small
sweet
tall
ugly
verbs
grow
swim
watch
expressions
what's the
matter?

8 Henry's holiday

nouns
back
blanket
bowl
camera
car
countryside
cream
Henry
holiday
ice cream
lizard

mountain
neck
rain
rainbow
rock
sand
shell
shower
snail
snow
soup
tablet
tent
torch
TV
village
weather
adjectives
boring
bad
hot
nice
wet
windy
verbs
snore
bring
give
read
stand

Acknowledgements

The author would like to acknowledge the shared professionalism and FUN she's experienced whilst working with colleagues during 20 years of production of YLE tests. She would also like to thank CUP for their support in the writing of this second edition of Storyfun.

On a personal note, Karen fondly thanks her inspirational story-telling grandfather, and now, three generations later, her sons, Tom and Will, for adding so much creative fun to our continuation of the family story-telling and story-making tradition.

The author and publishers would like to thank the following ELT professionals who commented on the material at different stages of development: Michelle and Silvia Ahmet Caldelas (Spain); Iain Kemp (Spain); Idalia Luz (Portugal); An Nguyen (Vietnam); Alice Soydas (Turkey); Sarah Walker (Spain).

Design and typeset by Wild Apple Design.

Cover design and header artwork by Nicholas Jackson (Astound).

Editing by Vicky Bewick.

Audio production by Hart McLeod, Cambridge.

Music by Mark Fishlock and produced by Ian Harker. Recorded at The Soundhouse Studios, London.

The authors and publishers acknowledge the following sources of copyright material and are grateful for the permissions granted. While every effort has been made, it has not always been possible to identify the sources of all the material used, or to trace all copyright holders. If any omissions are brought to our notice, we will be happy to include the appropriate acknowledgements on reprinting.

The publishers are grateful to the following for permission to reproduce copyright photographs and material:

Key: BL = Below Left, BR = Below Right, CL = Centre Left, CR = Centre Right, T = Top, TC = Top Centre, TL = Top Left, TR = Top Right.

p. 68 (T): Alex Bramwell/Moment/Getty Images; p. 69 (B): Stefan Cioata/Moment Open/Getty Images; p. 69 (grass): Rebecca Crabtree/Wild Apple Design; p. 71 (sky): Dougal Waters/DigitalVision/Getty Images; p. 72 (TR): Lane Oatey/Blue Jean Images/Getty Images; p. 72 (BL): Darrin Henry/iStock/Getty Images Plus/Getty Images; p. 72 (BR): Image Source/Image Source/Getty Images; p. 73 (TR): Lisa F. Young/iStock/Getty Images Plus/Getty Images; p. 73 (BL): Radius Images/Radius Images/Getty Images Plus/Getty Images; p. 73 (BR): Lori Adamski Peek/The Image Bank/Getty Images.

The following photographs on pages p. 72 (TL) and p. 73 (TL) were taken on commission by ©Stephen Bond and Trevor Clifford Photography for Cambridge University Press.

The authors and publishers are grateful to the following illustrators:

Chiara Buccheri (Lemonade) pp. 36, 37, 38, 39, 40, 41, 42, 43, 75 (TL); Ray and Corinne Burrows (Beehive Illustration) pp. 21 (B), 74 (BL); Nigel Dobbyn (Beehive Illustration) pp. 68 (BL), 71 (T); Fatemeh Haghnejad (Astound) pp. 52, 53, 54, 55, 56, 57, 58, 59, 75 (BL); Dave Kurtz Williams (Bright) pp. 48 (T), 75 (TR); Bonnie Pang (Astound) pp. 28, 29, 30, 31, 32, 33, 34, 35, 74 (BR); Esther Pérez-Cuadrado (Beehive Illustration) pp. 4, 5, 6, 7, 8, 9, 10, 11, 74 (TL); Melanie Sharp (Sylvie Poggio Artists Agency) pp. 60, 61, 62, 63, 64, 65, 66, 67, 75 (BR); Simon Smith (Beehive Illustration) pp. 12, 13, 14, 15, 16, 17, 18, 19, 74 (TR); Sarah Warburton pp. 20, 21, 22, 23, 24, 25, 26, 27; Cherie Zamazing pp. 44, 45, 46, 47, 48, 49, 50, 51, 75 (TR).